LIONS

LIVING WILD

Published by Creative Education
P.O. Box 227, Mankato, Minnesota 56002
Creative Education is an imprint of The Creative Company

Design and production by Mary Herrmann
Art direction by Rita Marshall
Printed in the United States of America

Photographs by Dreamstime (Ecophoto, Eromaze, Sekernas, Socrates), Getty Images (Altrendo Nature, Adrian Bailey/Aurora, A. Bayley-Worthington, Skip Brown, Nicole Duplaix, Gerald Hinde, Beverly Joubert, Yva Momatiuk/John Eastcott, Oxford Scientific/Photolibrary, Roman, Jonathan and Angela Scott, Anup Shah, Don Smith, Paul Sounders, Joseph Van Os, Art Wolfe), The Granger Collection, New York (Milo Winter), iStockphoto (Ballesta, Joe Brandt, John Carvalho, David Gomez, Bill Grove, Jonathan Heger, Claudiu Mazilu, David Ohrndorf, Nico Smit, Werner Van Peppen, Smirnov Vasily, Duncan Walker, Mark Wilson, WinterWitch, Igor Zhorov), NASA (Daniel Verschatse/Antilhue Observatory)

Library of Congress Cataloging-in-Publication Data
Hanel, Rachael.
Lions / by Rachael Hanel.
p. cm. — (Living wild)
Includes index.
ISBN 978-1-58341-656-3
1. Lions—Juvenile literature. I. Title. II. Series.

QL737.C23H352 2008
599.757—dc22   2007008504

First Edition
9 8 7 6 5 4 3 2 1

 CREATIVE EDUCATION

LIONS

Rachael Hanel

The sleek, muscular lioness
waits patiently in the tall grass.

The sleek, muscular lioness waits patiently in the tall grass. For several minutes, she has kept her eyes on the antelopes pausing at the watering hole. She is hungry and ready to eat. The antelopes have no idea she is hiding there. She creeps closer to her prey on padded paws, barely making a sound. Her brown fur blends perfectly with the color of the grass. When she is certain they still cannot see her, she takes a wild leap and pounces on one of the smaller antelopes. The other antelopes quickly run away. The one she has caught will be her meal. But first, she must let the male lions in her **pride** eat. Then she and the other females will eat, and the cubs will take whatever is left. The female's hunt satisfies the bellies of the pride for a few more days.

WHERE IN THE WORLD THEY LIVE

African Lion
sub-Saharan
Africa as far south
as South Africa

Asiatic Lion
northwestern India

Two species, African and
Asiatic, make up the entire
population of the world's lions
today. As represented by the
colored squares, lions can be
found in their native lands
of Africa and northwestern
India's Gir Forest.

KING OF BEASTS

The lion is the second-largest member of the Felidae, or cat, family, which also includes house cats, tigers, and cougars. All cats share such similar physical characteristics as whiskers, tails, and padded paws with **retractable** claws. The lion's closest relatives in the cat family are the leopard and cheetah. The lion's scientific name is *Panthera leo*.

More so than most other cats, the lion possesses a strength and power rarely seen in the animal kingdom. A lion shares its habitat with other large animals such as giraffes, hippopotamuses, and wildebeests, so it must be strong enough to compete with—and prey upon—these animals for survival.

A male African lion stands about four feet tall (1.2 m) and weighs around 420 pounds (198 kg). A female is smaller, standing a little shorter and weighing around 275 pounds (125 kg). The other main lion species, the rare Asiatic lion, is slightly smaller than the African lion and is found in parts of India.

All lions are covered with fur that can vary from yellow to dark brown. This color helps to **camouflage**

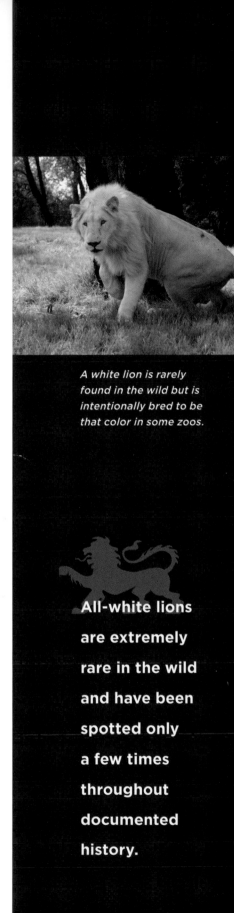

A white lion is rarely found in the wild but is intentionally bred to be that color in some zoos.

All-white lions are extremely rare in the wild and have been spotted only a few times throughout documented history.

the lion when it hunts for food. A lion has two coats of fur. Close to the skin, a soft, light layer helps insulate and protect the skin. The outer, visible layer consists of tough, wiry hairs that guard the lion against sharp branches, other animals' claws, and fierce wind and rain.

The male lion's most recognizable physical feature is the thick, bushy mane that encircles its head and neck. The hair found in the mane is much thicker and longer than the stiff hair covering the rest of the lion's body. A lion's mane can grow up to 20 inches (51 cm) long. Sometimes the mane is the same color as the rest of the body, but it can also be black, dark brown, or range in shades of gray to orange.

Because lions hunt at night, they have **keen** eyesight that enables them to find and track prey in the dark. The **pupils** of their eyes get very large at night to let in all available light. Stiff whiskers on the sides of their noses also help them navigate through the darkness. If their whiskers brush up against a tree, lions know they need to move over to avoid bumping into it.

A lion's bushy tail, which often swishes back and forth as it walks, helps it keep its balance. It also aids in

Lionesses work together to round up larger prey, but sometimes they are chased themselves.

Lion cubs are playful and can get away with gnawing on adult lions' tails to help improve their teeth.

communication, helping lions to spot each other from far away. The tail, like the mane, is composed of longer hair. The **tuft** of hair at the tail's end is unique to the lion. This black patch of fur helps lions see each other in the tall grass.

All parts of a lion are thickly muscled, especially the back legs. This enables the big cat to leap several feet forward when pouncing upon its prey. A lion's paws look like larger versions of paws seen on house cats. Pads on the bottom of the paw help a lion to move about quietly, especially when stalking prey. When a lion walks, its claws are hidden. But when it's ready to kill its prey, the lion uses special muscles in its paws to extend its claws. The front paws have five claws, and the back paws have four. Lions also use their claws to get a better grip on the ground when they run. Scratching tree trunks helps a lion keep its claws sharp.

Lions survive on a diet of meat, and they need a variety of teeth to chew their food. All lions have 30 teeth. The front teeth, called **canines**, look like curved fangs. These are the longest teeth and are two and a half to three inches (6.4–7.6 cm) long. A lion has two canines on the

Any time prey is killed, the male lions in a pride eat their fill first.

Lions will stop at a pond or river to take a drink, but, like most cats, they do not like to swim unless they have to.

If a lion's canine teeth are damaged, it will be harder for it to catch prey.

A lion's deep, bellowing roar can be heard up to five miles (8.1 km) away. Males roar louder and much more often than females.

top and two on the bottom. These teeth help a lion grab and hold on to its prey. Toward the back of a lion's mouth are four **carnassial** teeth, two on the top and two on the bottom. These teeth are jagged and help a lion tear through meat. Molars at the back of the mouth grind the meat. To clean flesh from bones, a lion's rough tongue acts like a piece of sandpaper. The cat also uses its tongue to keep its fur clean, and lions often will groom each other with their tongues.

Lions used to live throughout Africa, Europe, the Middle East, and southern Asia. But today, lions are found only in Africa and in one small part of Asia, the protected Gir Forest in northwestern India. Even in Africa, lions live in only a few dozen spots throughout the vast continent and are rarely found outside of protected reserves. It is not known exactly how many lions are in Africa, but estimates range from 23,000 to 30,000. Only about 350 Asiatic lions live in the Gir Forest.

In Africa, lions can be found from the southern edge of the Sahara Desert in the north to South Africa, near the continent's southern tip. Countries in which lions live include Kenya, Tanzania, Zambia, and Angola. Despite

While antelopes drink at a watering hole, lions will plot how best to sneak up on them.

their "king of the jungle" nickname, lions do not live in the wet, tropical forests found in the west-central part of the continent. They prefer grassy plains with trees and shrubs—areas called savannas—or woodsy, dry forests. Lions like to have places to hide, such as behind trees or large rocks, when stalking their prey or protecting newborn cubs. Lions also like to climb on top of hills or rocks to survey the land around them.

Lions need plenty of space in which to live. Their territories may be as small as 25 square miles (65 sq km) or as large as 250 square miles (648 sq km), depending on the availability of prey within the area. Their territory must include a water source such as a pond, lake, or river. These watering holes also attract other animals upon which lions prey.

Male and female lions are polygamous, meaning that they have many different mating partners.

A FAMILY AFFAIR

Lions depend on family to survive. Lions live in groups called prides, which consist of males, females, and their young. Prides can be as small as just one male and perhaps two females, or as large as 30 lions total, but most groups have around 15 members. All females in a pride are related—mothers and daughters, cousins, aunts, and nieces. Female cubs born into a pride generally will stay with that pride, but male cubs will leave to join other prides.

The daily routine of a lion is largely uneventful. Lions sleep or rest for up to 20 hours a day. This helps them stay cool in the heat, and it also helps them conserve their energy for more important activities such as mating and hunting.

Mating occurs within the pride. But the animals do not always have the same partner and may mate many times with different lions. There is no particular mating season for lions, but all the females in the pride tend to mate around the same time. A female gives birth to cubs about three and a half months after mating. When she is ready to have her babies, she finds an isolated, dry place—such as a shady spot underneath a tree or between large rocks—to

All members of a lion pride carry a common smell that they pass on to each other by rubbing their heads together.

use as a den. Her **litter** consists of two to six cubs.

When lion cubs are born, they are so tiny it is hard
to believe they will grow into such large, magnificent
creatures. They weigh only two to four pounds (.9–1.8
kg) at birth. Cubs are born with spotted orange and
brown fur, which helps them remain hidden in the grass.
These spots fade as the cubs grow up. The youngsters

will stay in the den near their mother for a few weeks.
Their eyes remain shut for more than a week, and they do
nothing but nurse for up to eight hours a day. The mother
stays close to her cubs to protect them and gently licks
them clean so that their scent will not attract predators.
She and the other mothers will leave their young only to
find food and water. They leave all the cubs together, and

Cubs find a shady spot in which they can keep cool and hidden while their mothers are gone.

For the first few weeks of their lives, cubs get their food in the form of their mothers' milk.

Only about half of all cubs born will reach adulthood. The rest fall to disease, predators, or attacks from adult lions.

the cubs instinctively know to remain quiet in order not to alert predators to their presence.

When the cubs are about five weeks old, they follow their mothers out of the den to join the rest of the pride. There, they playfully swipe at and chase each other. This playtime looks like fun, but the cubs are actually learning important skills that they will use when it is time for them to chase their own prey. When the cubs join the pride, they start to eat meat. At first, they eat the meat of animals that other lions have killed. It takes a long time for young lions to learn how to hunt, and they do not do it on their own until they are about 15 months old.

When young male lions are about two years old, they are ready to leave the pride. Brothers will generally stay together while searching for a new home. A group of males looking for a pride is called a coalition. Coalitions find prides by tracking the scent of other lions. To mark a territory, a lion urinates on or rubs against trees and bushes.

Once a coalition finds a pride, the competition from males that are there already can be fierce, and fighting usually ensues. Males work hard to defend their pride and territory. Sometimes they can drive a rival coalition away. But eventually, a coalition finds a pride with weak males and takes over. When males take over a pride, they sometimes kill the existing cubs in order to build a pride that has only their own offspring.

All lions move around their territory together to search for prey. Lions most often prey upon wildebeests, zebras, gazelles, antelopes, wild pigs, and warthogs. If a lion feels especially brave, it may attack the young of much larger animals such as giraffes and hippopotamuses. With a lion's power and strength, it may seem that few animals stand a chance against such an attack. But many of the animals that lions prey upon have the ability to run very quickly. A lion can run up to 40 miles (64 km) per hour but only for short distances. A lion may bring down a meal in only one out of every six tries.

Hunting usually falls to the females of a pride. They are leaner than males and move much more gracefully and quickly through the grass. Sometimes females will hunt by themselves, but often they hunt in groups. That way, they can sneak up on their prey and quietly encircle it. At the moment of attack, the group of females can run down the slower and weaker animals. A lion kills its prey by

A pair of lionesses often has more success in hunting prey.

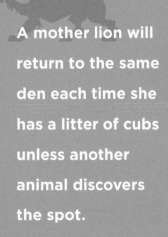

A mother lion will return to the same den each time she has a litter of cubs unless another animal discovers the spot.

Lionesses will scatter a herd of larger
animals (such as water buffalo) and chase
the weaker ones.

clamping onto the throat with its teeth and suffocating it.

After a kill, the entire pride gathers around the **carcass**, and each lion competes for its share. Generally, the males in the pride eat first, then the females, then the cubs. Lions will eat as much as possible at once because they never know when their next meal will be. Lions also eat carrion—animals that have died or been killed by other predators. Sometimes lions use their size and power to scare off smaller animals, such as hyenas, that might be eating a fresh kill.

Lions are at the top of the food chain in the African **ecosystem**, and grown lions have no natural predators. However, their cubs are vulnerable to attack from leopards and hyenas, and adult lions can be injured when chasing prey. For example, animals such as zebras and antelopes have sharp hooves that can cut and seriously injure lions. Lions can maim each other as well, especially when males are fighting to dominate a pride. Humans also pose a danger to lions, as ranchers and hunters sometimes illegally kill the big animals. In the wild, lions can live for about 12 to 16 years, but their life expectancy increases to 25 years in captivity.

In many cultures, lions such as this one from China were a symbol of a leader's power and strength.

A SYMBOL OF POWER

L ions have always fascinated humans. Lions walk and carry themselves with dignity and grace, and they have become associated with these qualities. Lions also represent strength, courage, and bravery. The lion is often said to be the "king" of all animals because of its position at the top of the food chain.

Lions have been used as important symbols for centuries. Images of the animals graced flags and **heraldry** of high-ranking European families. Representations of lions can also be found wherever they once lived. Images of prehistoric lions have been located in ancient Indian and African art and even in the caves of southern France.

In the Roman Empire of about 2,000 years ago and in later kingdoms and cultures, lions were featured in popular **gladiator** contests. Emperors and kings, along with thousands of bloodthirsty spectators, watched as lions fought each other and humans for sport. Later, poets such as James Henry Leigh Hunt recounted such tales in verse.

By the first century A.D., lions started to disappear from Europe as the human population **infringed** on their territories and competed for their food. The lion's

A famous king of England, Richard I, was called "Richard the Lionhearted" for his bravery and courage when fighting in 12th-century battles.

Alexander the Great was a legendary military leader who controlled a powerful and large kingdom.

range shifted eastward, and it lived in eastern Europe's Caucasus Mountains until the 10th century. The Asiatic lion once roamed from Turkey throughout the Middle East to India. But aggressive hunting took its toll on the populations of these lions. By the late 19th century, the Asiatic lion had disappeared from Turkey, and lions were last seen in Iran in the mid–20th century.

Lion hunting remained a popular sport for centuries. People who were able to kill a lion were believed to have unusual courage and bravery. Important figures in ancient history, such as Greek ruler Alexander the Great and Egyptian pharaoh Rameses II were thought to have hunted lions and kept some as pets. Throughout history, African tribesmen killed lions to prove that they were no longer boys but men.

As people began to travel the world with greater ease starting in the 17th century, more were drawn to Africa for its unusual creatures and adventurous **safari** hunts. On these trips, hunters would kill lions, preserve their bodies or heads, and take them home to display as trophies of their hunting skills. When the gun was introduced in the 18th and 19th centuries, lion populations suffered larger

THE GLOVE AND THE LIONS

King Francis was a hearty king, and loved a
    royal sport,
And one day, as his lions fought, sat looking on
    the court.
The nobles filled the benches, and the ladies in
    their pride,
And 'mongst them sat the Count de Lorge, with
    one for whom he sighed:
And truly 'twas a gallant thing to see that
    crowning show,
Valor and love, and a king above, and the royal
    beasts below.

Ramped and roared the lions, with horrid
    laughing jaws;
They bit, they glared, gave blows like beams, a
    wind went with their paws;
With wallowing might and stifled roar they rolled
    on one another,
Till all the pit with sand and mane was in a
    thunderous smother;
The bloody foam above the bars came whisking
    through the air;
Said Francis then, "Faith, gentlemen, we're
    better here than there."

De Lorge's love o'erheard the King, a beauteous
    lively dame,
With smiling lips and sharp bright eyes, which
    always seemed the same;
She thought, the Count my lover is brave as
    brave can be;
He surely would do wondrous things to show his
    love of me;
King, ladies, lovers, all look on; the occasion
    is divine;
I'll drop my glove, to prove his love; great glory
    will be mine.

She dropped her glove, to prove his love, then
    looked at him and smiled;
He bowed, and in a moment leaped among the
    lions wild:
The leap was quick, return was quick, he has
    regained his place,
Then threw the glove, but not with love, right in
    the lady's face.
"By Heaven," said Francis, "rightly done!" and
    he rose from where he sat:
"No love," quoth he, "but vanity, sets love a task
    like that."

James Henry Leigh Hunt (1784–1859)

In Africa's Serengeti National Park, lions are free to run and roam without fear of being hunted.

declines than ever before. In 1909, former United States president Teddy Roosevelt went on a yearlong safari with his son. In 12 months, they killed 500 big game animals, including 17 lions, and brought specimens back to display at the Smithsonian Institution in Washington, D.C.

Unfortunately, lion populations continue to decline today. The Asiatic lion is endangered, and the World Conservation Union has given the African lion "vulnerable" status, meaning it is close to becoming endangered. The organization estimates that there has been a 30 to 50 percent decline in the lion population in the last two decades. In specific regions, such as West Africa, the lion is considered endangered, with the number of mating lions estimated to be around 1,000.

Due to their declining numbers, the majority of lions now live within the protected confines of national parks. Countries in which lions live often contain several spacious parks. Serengeti National Park in the eastern African country of Tanzania encompasses 5,100 square miles (15,000 sq km), and all the animals and habitats within it are protected. It is not unusual to see large numbers of lions on a drive through the park, even

If they are unable to find another pride with which to share food, male lions that are driven out of prides may die within a few months.

When ancient astronomers looked at the night sky, they saw stars that seemed to form the shape of a lion, and they named the constellation "Leo."

though they are endangered. Such preserves can give visitors a false impression about overall lion populations.

Lions have always been important to the native peoples of Africa and Asia, but it was not until lions were taken out of their natural habitats that people around the world got their first look at the giant cats. Lions soon captured the imaginations of many and found their way into popular culture in different ways.

For centuries, lions were a regular circus feature. But it wasn't until the 17th century in England that circuses featured "lion-tamers." These daring men and women would perform in the same ring or cage as lions and make the animals jump, leap, and perform tricks. Unfortunately, many lion-tamers remembered too late that they were working with wild animals, and careless tamers were injured or killed. The best-known lion-tamer was Gunther Gebel-Williams, who worked for the Ringling Bros. and Barnum & Bailey Circus in the mid-20th century.

In literature, perhaps the most famous lion character appears in British author C. S. Lewis's children's tale, *The Lion, the Witch, and the Wardrobe*. In this 1950 book, a lion named Aslan is the strongest animal in the kingdom of

Although lions once lived in northern Europe and Asia, today they appear in colder regions only in zoos.

Lions can be found in art and architecture around the world, symbolically guarding the entrance to such buildings as temples, castles, and churches.

Narnia, though he has been absent for many years. He returns in time to save four children—who had entered the kingdom through a magical wardrobe—from the evil White Witch. The witch kills Aslan, but he comes back to life to peacefully rule the kingdom. The book has been made into cartoons and a 2005 Hollywood movie.

Perhaps the best-known fictional lion of recent years is the cub Simba, from the Disney animated movie *The Lion King.* Simba battles with his uncle, Scar, to take over his rightful place as the head of the pride. Even though the movie does not accurately mirror reality (male cubs usually leave to find a new pride), the movie delighted audiences and inspired a Broadway play.

With their imposing and proud manner, lions make for popular mascots. A roaring lion can be seen before the start of every film made by the Metro-Goldwyn-Mayer (MGM) movie company. The fierce, competitive lion makes a fitting mascot for many sports teams as well, including the Detroit Lions of the National Football League.

Lions remain a beloved animal among the public, and they are the main reason why many people travel to Africa and go on safari. Seeing a lion in the wild is considered a chance of a lifetime for many people, and the countries in which lions live benefit economically from the tourism lions and other wildlife bring.

Apart from making a male look bigger and more imposing, a full, dark mane attracts females.

THE LION TODAY

Only the strongest lions survive the longest, and young males will fight to prove their dominance.

Because the lion is one of the world's most fascinating creatures, scientists have been driven to study its origins, behaviors, and characteristics for many years. Today's lions can be traced back to larger lions that once lived throughout the Northern and Southern Hemispheres. Remains of North American lions have been located as far north as Alaska and as far south as the South American border. In Europe, the cave lion lived millions of years ago. Fossils have also been discovered that suggest the existence of a **marsupial** lion in Australia that died off about 30,000 years ago. The Asiatic lion is thought to have split from the African lion about 100,000 years ago.

Scientists first started studying lions in the 1960s. That early research centered on lion behavior, such as why lions are the only feline to live in social groups and why and how they cooperate with each other. Current lion research focuses on ways to conserve the lion population and help it grow. Scientists think they can do this by concentrating on the issues of reproduction, communication, and habitat.

A lioness's fierce nature makes attaching a tracking device tricky.

In rare cases, a male lion will not grow a mane. This could mean he is not as healthy as other males with manes.

Scientists track lions to provide estimates of their populations and to watch for the slightest decrease in numbers so they can prevent further declines. Researchers monitor lions by fitting a female with a tracking device. Because lions live in prides, monitoring one lion in each pride is usually sufficient. The females lead the researchers to other lions within the pride. Researchers come to recognize each individual lion through a unique pattern of dots that are near its whiskers. These dots are like human fingerprints, and each lion sports a different pattern. Scientists monitor the animals every few days to note any changes in a lion's appearance, behavior, or health.

Recent research has also centered on lions' manes. Theories abound as to why male lions have manes. They are the only cats with a mane, and they are the only cats that live in groups, so scientists assume the mane plays some important social role. The condition of the mane can indicate a lion's health, with thick, dark hair signifying a healthier, stronger lion. If one male appears weak, another male may be more willing to fight for control of a pride or for a female's attention.

The darker the lion's mane is, the better chance he has of fathering healthy, playful cubs.

A lion family is close until mature cubs have to leave the pride to start new families of their own.

Using life-sized stuffed animals, one team of researchers set out to discover what purpose the mane served. Each of the four fake lions had different manes, varying from light to dark and from short to long. In most cases, female lions preferred the lion with the long, dark mane. Testing real lions with dark manes, scientists found that those males had a higher amount of testosterone, a hormone present in all males. The higher the levels, the more attractive the male was to a female. A healthy male also had a better chance of fathering healthy cubs.

Scientists also monitor lions in parks and reserves for genetic problems that can result from **inbreeding**. If a

pride is isolated and small, family members will mate
with each other and produce offspring that may be sick
or weak. In these cases, scientists may try to artificially
inseminate lions or introduce new females into the pride
to maintain genetic diversity.

The lion still faces many threats to its population,
including those posed by disease. In the early 1990s,
one-third of all lions in Serengeti National Park died
from canine distemper, a disease found in dogs that lived
in the villages surrounding the park. Research showed
the disease was passed from dogs to hyenas, which then
traveled long distances and came into contact with lions.

Lions can climb trees. Often they will rest on limbs high above the ground to avoid annoying insects that buzz in the grass.

Since then, dogs in those African villages have been vaccinated to halt the spread of the deadly disease.

Perhaps the biggest threat to lions today is humans. In areas where lions are not protected, they are vulnerable to the destruction of habitat that occurs when the human population grows. In Africa, land for cattle and other ranch animals is in high demand. As the agricultural industry continues to expand, the lion's habitat will continue to shrink.

Human imposition upon the habitat also affects the populations of zebras, wildebeests, antelopes, and other prey upon which lions depend. Lions, in a desperate search for food, sometimes attack cattle on nearby ranches, leading ranchers to shoot the lions. Ranchers are allowed to shoot lions that attack cattle, but sometimes they end up killing innocent lions as well. Snares and traps used to catch other animals can accidentally entangle lions, and they sometimes choke to death or are gravely injured.

In some countries, lion hunting is legal but limited to a certain number of licenses per year. For example, the government of Botswana allows a limited number of **trophy hunters** to come in each year and shoot lions. But in the majority of countries where it is illegal to hunt lions, **poaching** continues. An underground animal parts trade exists, in which the skin, bones, and other parts of exotic animals are traded and sold for profit.

Today, there are many measures in place to protect the lion. For example, the Walt Disney Foundation supports Project Simba (named after *The Lion King* character), which helps scientists work with local populations to save lions in Kenya. Scientists who have researched problems facing lions advise native Maasai ranchers to build stronger enclosures that will keep their cattle safe—and keep the ranchers from killing more lions.

Many organizations and researchers spend large amounts of time and money on efforts to conserve the lion populations and help them grow. The number of healthy lions is linked to the population of all other animals in Africa. If lions suffer, other animals are bound to suffer, too. The more aware the world is about lions and their questionable future, the more people can join to help save one of Earth's most majestic creatures.

Several organizations around the world work to ensure that lions are able to live in the wild safely.

ANIMAL TALE: THE LION AND THE MOUSE

It is not surprising that the lion, with its imposing stature, kingly roar, and graceful good looks, is the subject of many legends throughout Africa and beyond. The following tale is credited to Aesop, a Greek citizen who lived in the sixth century B.C., at a time when lions were a common sight in Greece. Aesop wrote a number of stories called fables that featured animals and taught important life lessons. The moral of the lion and the mouse is that people never know when they might need a friend, so it is a good idea to treat everyone kindly.

One day, a great lion was taking a nap in the shade of a big tree. Soon, a little mouse started running up and down the lion's body. The lion awoke with a start. He pinned the mouse with a paw and glared at it.

"What are you doing?" the lion roared. "Don't you know who I am? I am the greatest beast in the world. How dare you scamper all over me and disturb my sleep?"

The mouse was greatly afraid and trembled as he spoke. "I'm so sorry, Lion. I didn't mean to bother you. I was only playing and accidentally stumbled onto you."

"I should eat you right now!" the lion shouted, opening his mouth wide.

"Oh, no, please don't eat me!" the mouse begged. "Really, I am truly sorry. Please let me go, and I promise it will be worthwhile. I will be your friend forever. Perhaps I may be of some help to you someday."

The lion laughed at the thought. "You, a little mouse, help me, a giant lion? That's about the silliest idea I've ever heard. But you make me laugh, so I'll let you go. I'm warning you, don't bother me again!"

"Oh, thank you so much, Lion!" said the mouse, greatly relieved. "I promise, you won't be sorry!"

The mouse scurried away, and the lion continued with his nap.

Several months later, the lion was walking through the forest when he stepped in a hunter's net. The net closed tightly around him, and the more he struggled, the more tangled he became. He roared and roared, but no amount of noise could free him.

However, the mouse heard the lion's cries for help and came running to him.

"Lion, I'm here!" said the mouse. "I can save you from this net." The mouse used his sharp teeth to cut the netting, and soon the lion was free.

"Oh, you saved my life!" the lion said. "I can't thank you enough. You were right; even something as small as you are could help something as big as I am." And the lion and the mouse remained good friends for many years.

GLOSSARY

camouflage – the ability to hide, due to coloring or markings that blend in with a given environment

canines – long front teeth that resemble fangs

carcass – the dead body of an animal

carnassial – a flat tooth found toward the back of the upper and lower jaw that is used to grind meat and bone

ecosystem – a community of organisms, plants, and animals that live together in an environment

gladiator – an ancient Roman fighter who performed in front of large crowds, often fighting until he was killed in the arena

heraldry – images, often used on medieval flags, that identified one family from another and held personal meaning for the family

inbreeding – the mating of individuals that are closely related; it can result in offspring with genetic problems

infringed – when someone has gone beyond the usual limit and intruded upon someone else's space

inseminate – to place a male's sperm and a female's eggs together in order for a baby to grow in the female's womb

keen – sharp and perceptive; having the ability to draw small distinctions between objects

litter – babies that are born at the same time to animals such as dogs, cats, lions, and tigers

marsupial – an animal, such as a koala or kangaroo, that has a pouch in which its young can grow and mature

poaching – illegally hunting and killing protected species of fish or game

pride – a group of lions that travel and live together in a pack; it consists of males, females, and cubs

pupils – the dark parts of the eye that expand or contract to let in sufficient light

retractable – having the ability to draw back

safari – a journey undertaken by hunters in search of big game; the word means "trip" in the African Swahili language

trophy hunters – people who strive to kill large or unusual game and keep the body—or parts of it—to display

tuft – an extension of feathers or hair that usually forms a ridge or fluffy ball

SELECTED BIBLIOGRAPHY

Corrigan, Patricia, Kathy Feeney, Gwyneth Swain, and Cherie Winner. *Big Cats*. Chanhassen, Minn.: NorthWord Press, 2002.

Holmes, Kevin J. *Lions*. Mankato, Minn.: Bridgestone Books, 1999.

Public Broadcasting System. "The Vanishing Lions." Nature. http://www.pbs.org/wnet/nature/vanishinglions/.

Smithsonian Institution. "Great Cats: Lion Facts." National Zoological Park. http://nationalzoo.si.edu/Animals/GreatCats/lionfacts.cfm.

Spilsbury, Louise, and Richard Spilsbury. *Watching Lions in Africa*. Chicago: Heinemann Library, 2006.

University of Michigan Museum of Zoology. "Panthera Leo (Lion)." Animal Diversity Web. http://animaldiversity.ummz.umich.edu/site/accounts/information/Panthera_leo.hml.

Lionesses in the same pride will often watch over cubs that are not their own while others hunt.

INDEX